VICTORIANS

CLARE CHANDLER

ILLUSTRATED BY JESSICA CURTIS

Wayland

HISTORY MAKERS

Notes for teachers

History Makers uses a wide range of exciting contemporary sources – quotations, letters, paintings and artefacts – to build up detailed and informative portraits of people who made important contributions both to their own time and to the way we live now.

This book:

- features important figures from all areas of Victorian life – science and technology, the arts, exploration, war, education and health;

- presents contemporary reactions to changes and innovations;

- focuses on Victorian society and the reforms that were introduced to improve the lives of many people;

- emphasizes the importance of Victorian achievements for modern life.

First published in 1994 by Wayland
(Publishers) Ltd
61 Western Road, Hove, East Sussex
BN3 1JD, England

© Copyright 1994 Wayland (Publishers) Ltd

Series editor: Katie Roden
Series designer: Tracy Gross
Book designer: Joyce Chester

British Library Cataloguing in Publication Data

Chandler, Clare
Victorians. – (History Makers Series)
I. Title   II. Curtis, Jessica   III. Series
941.081

ISBN 0-7502-1267-5

Typeset by Dorchester Typesetting Group
Ltd, England
Printed and bound in Italy by Lego

Picture acknowledgements

Bristol Museum and Art Gallery 18, 19 (both); British Film Institute Stills, Posters and Designs 31 (bottom); Brontë Parsonage Museum 36; Brunel University Library 20; Down House/The Royal College of Surgeons of England 24 (bottom); Mary Evans Picture Library 7, (top), 16, 17, 24 (top); John Freeman 27; Girton College, Cambridge 38, 40; Guildhall Library, London 18; Hulton Deutsch 8, 23; Imperial War Museum 15; National Portrait Gallery 37; Newnham College, Cambridge 39; Royal Commonwealth Society Library 43; Royal Photographic Society 22, 33 (top), 34, 35; Science Museum 21; Trinity College, Cambridge 42 (both); Wayland Picture Library 6, 7 (bottom), 9, 11, 12, 25, 26, 29 (both), 30, 31 (top), 32, 33 (bottom), 41 (both).

Contents

Words in **bold** in the text can be found in the Glossary on page 44.

Elizabeth Fry

1780 - 1845

'*They occupied two long rooms, where they slept in three tiers, some on the floor and two tiers of hammocks over one another... When I first entered the foulness of the air was almost insupportable; ... On going up, I was astonished beyond description at the mass of woe and misery I beheld. I found many very sick, lying on the bare floor or on some old straw, having very scanty covering over them, though it was quite cold; and there were several children born in the prison among them, almost naked.*'

So wrote Stephen Grellet, an American visiting the women's area of Newgate Prison in London on a bitingly cold winter day in 1813. He then visited his friend and fellow **Quaker**, Elizabeth Fry, at her home,

Mrs Fry's reforms started here at Newgate Prison in London. She believed that 'Punishment is not for revenge, but to lessen crime and reform the criminal.'

6

and described to her what he had seen. The very next day Mrs Fry went to the prison herself with bundles of clothes that she and some friends had made for the children. The misery that she found there inspired a project that would be her life's work and would change conditions in prisons not only in Britain but also across Europe.

Visiting time at a London prison. The prisoners hardly ever saw their friends or family.

Elizabeth Fry had always wanted to help people who were less fortunate than herself. Growing up in a large, happy, wealthy family in Norfolk, she was soon aware of the difference between her life and the lives of the local villagers. As soon as she was married and living on a large estate of her own, she began several projects to improve the lives of the local people. She founded a school for the children and started a soup kitchen in one of the barns to feed the poor. She **vaccinated** as many people as she could, keeping the area free of **smallpox**.

The better prisons had a yard like this where prisoners could exercise. Here, they have the type of wheel that is usually found in hamsters' cages.

7

Mrs Fry reading the *Bible* to prisoners. The effects of her reforms on the women at Newgate were dramatic. She said, 'Already, from being wild beasts, they appear harmless and kind.' Look closely at the picture – do you think all the prisoners are completely reformed?

Apart from her natural kindness, Elizabeth Fry was inspired to help people by her strong religious beliefs. Her family were Quakers but very relaxed. Unlike them, she was one of the 'plain' Quakers, who were very strict and disapproved of entertainments such as music and dancing. While her sisters had fashionable dresses with high waistlines and low necks, Elizabeth wore a simple dress with a natural waistline, a white scarf tied around her throat and a plain white cap.

Above all, Mrs Fry felt that if prisoners had useful things to do there would be an end to the fighting, drunkenness and other bad habits that were common in prison. She wanted to help the prisoners at Newgate to become better people. So she organized a school, letting the prisoners choose their own schoolmistress. The women were taught to read, write and sew. They could make clothes for themselves and patchwork quilts which could be sold to make a little money. The change was immediate and extraordinary. People who had visited the prison only a month before were astonished at the difference.

'They saw no more an assemblage (crowd) of abandoned and shameless creatures, half naked and half drunk ... This "hell upon earth" exhibited the appearance of an industrious manufactory or a well-regulated family.'

So wrote Mrs Fry's brother-in-law, Fowell Buxton. He was a **Member of Parliament** and was inspired by her to change the law about prisons.

8

At that time, many prisoners were simply transported from Britain to Australia. Elizabeth Fry tried to improve the terrible journey aboard the convict ships. She arranged classes for the women and schools for their children on board ship, and made sure that the women were allowed to take all their children under the age of seven with them.

Mrs Fry visited all the convict ships before they left for Australia – 106 ships in all – and improved the conditions for 12,000 convicts.

She was now famous for her work and was often asked for advice on prison reform by government committees. She did all this as well as bringing up eleven children of her own! You can see her popularity in this description by her daughter of Mrs Fry meeting Queen Charlotte, the wife of King George III:

'The shouts in the hall were tremendous, and were caught up by the crowds outside. It was told why they shouted, and it was repeated again and again, till it reached our father, sitting in his office ... "The Queen is speaking to Mrs Fry".'

OTHER PRISON REFORMERS

Sir Robert Peel
– a Conservative Prime Minister.
Dorothy Dix
– an American social reformer.

9

Michael Faraday

1791-1867

'His enthusiasm sometimes carried him to the point of ecstasy when he **expatiated** *on the beauty of nature, and when he lifted the veil from her deep mysteries. His body then took motion from his mind; his hair streamed out from his head, his hands were full of nervous action, his light lithe body seemed to quiver with its eager life. His audience took fire with him, and every face was flushed.'*

Michael Faraday was so passionate about science that he was a wonderful and inspiring teacher, as you can tell from this description of him by Lady Holland. His lectures at the Royal Institution became one of the great entertainments of Victorian London and helped to make science popular. When he lectured to children he was like a magician performing in front of them. He would demonstrate the power of the magnet by hurling a bucket of coals at the Royal Institution's great **electromagnet**. When it stuck there, he would throw the fire tongs and poker after it. He wanted to create the same excitement about the laws of nature that had been sparked in him as a boy. This had inspired him to be one of the great scientists of the world.

Faraday had to leave school at the age of thirteen. His father was a blacksmith and Michael had to go to work to help support his family. At first he worked as an errand boy, delivering newspapers for a bookseller. Because he was clever, he was employed as an **apprentice** bookbinder, learning how to bind books together and cover them. This gave him the opportunity to read and made him passionately keen to learn more. He started going to evening lectures, taking detailed notes which he later bound into books. After a series of lectures by Humphry Davy, Faraday showed the famous scientist the notes he had taken. Davy was so impressed that he took Faraday on as his assistant.

In this entry from his diary on 29 August 1831, Faraday set out clearly how he made his most famous discovery – electromagnetic induction.

For several years Faraday worked for Humphry Davy, experimenting in chemistry. However, during this time he became obsessed with electricity. There were two questions he wanted to answer: what was electricity, and how did it work? He did experiment after experiment until 1831, when he made his most important discovery, electromagnetic induction. He made electricity using just a magnet and a coil of wire. This was the basis of the first **dynamo**, the invention that has made modern civilization possible. Electromagnetic induction is used to make electricity today.

OTHER SCIENTISTS

Humphry Davy
– a chemist.
John Dalton
– a chemist and physicist.
André Marie Ampère
– a physicist and mathematician.
Alessandro Volta
– a physicist.

In honour of his discoveries, Faraday was asked to be president of the Royal Society and was offered a knighthood. But he refused both honours, saying, 'I must remain plain Michael Faraday to the last'.

A SCIENTIFIC CENTENARY.

Faraday (returned). "WELL, MISS SCIENCE, I HEARTILY CONGRATULATE YOU; YOU HAVE MADE MARVELLOUS PROGRESS SINCE MY TIME!"

This cartoon commemorating the centenary of Faraday's birth, in 1891, shows him admiring some of the advances science had made, including the telephone, since his death in 1867.

Discover electromagnetic induction for yourself.

You will need a cardboard toilet roll, a long piece of wire (at least one metre), a bar magnet and either a galvanometer or a compass.

1. Wind the wire around the toilet roll leaving at least 15 cm at each end. Make sure your coil is neat with no wires crossing over each other.

12

2. If you have a galvanometer, attach the two ends of the wire to it. If you have a compass, join the ends of the wire to each other and lay the compass over the join. You have now made a circuit.

3. Move the magnet in and out of the toilet roll and see what happens. If you make any electricity, the needle of the compass or galvanometer will wobble backwards and forwards slightly.

4. Try moving the magnet slowly then quickly and see if there is any difference.

DISCOVER ELECTROMAGNETIC INDUCTION

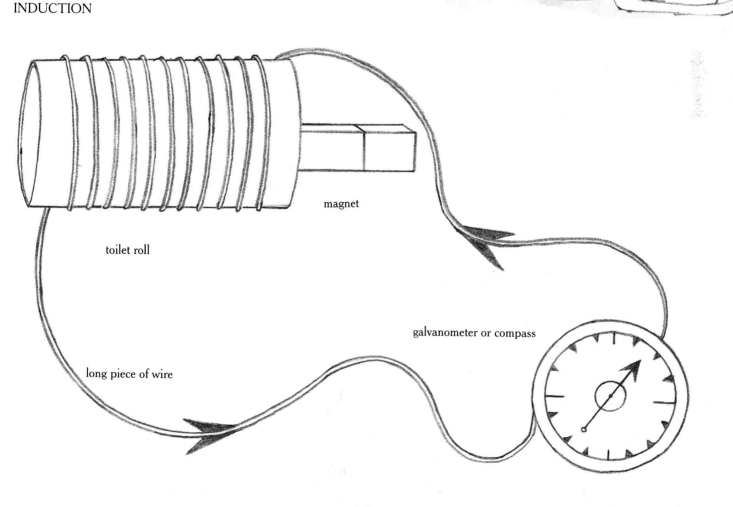

magnet

toilet roll

galvanometer or compass

long piece of wire

Mary Seacole

1805-1881

'The very first day that I approached the wharf (at Balaclava) a party of sick and wounded had just arrived... seeing a poor artilleryman... I ran up to him at once, and eased the stiff dressing... and well was I rewarded when the poor fellow's groans subsided into a restless easy mutter.'

Mary Seacole became famous in the Crimea for her kindness and skill at nursing the wounded soldiers.

She was born Mary Jane Grant in Kingston, Jamaica. Her mother was a free black woman (on an island where most black people were still slaves to white people), who ran a boarding house and worked as a doctor practising traditional Caribbean medicine. As a child Mary loved nursing and learnt about the treatment of tropical illnesses and wounds from her mother.

When the **Crimean War** broke out Mary decided to go and nurse the wounded there. She knew that the soldiers were kept in terrible conditions, made worse by the shortage of food, medicine and clothing. The hospitals were filthy and rat-infested and the people who did not die of battle wounds suffered from **cholera** and **malaria**. Mary first travelled from Jamaica to England to work as a nurse. But, despite her experience and letters of reference from doctors, she was turned down. She then tried to join Florence Nightingale's group of nurses to go to the Crimea, but again she was rejected. She wondered whether,

'these ladies shrink from accepting my aid because my blood flow(s) beneath a somewhat duskier skin than theirs?'

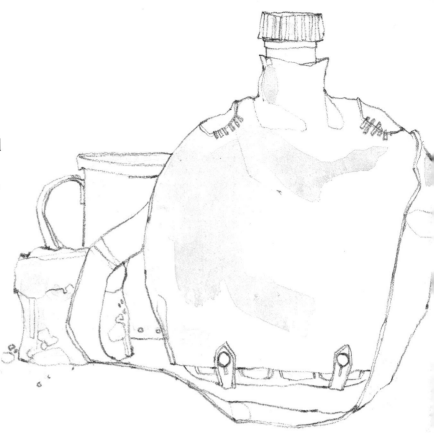

Soldiers in the Crimean War lived in tents like these, even when the snow was thick on the ground. They did not have enough food or clothing either.

However, she did not give up, and travelled to the Crimea by herself. With a partner, she set up as a **sutler**, selling food and drink to the army, and opened the British Hotel, providing healthy food for the soldiers. She achieved her ambition of nursing the wounded and sick men.

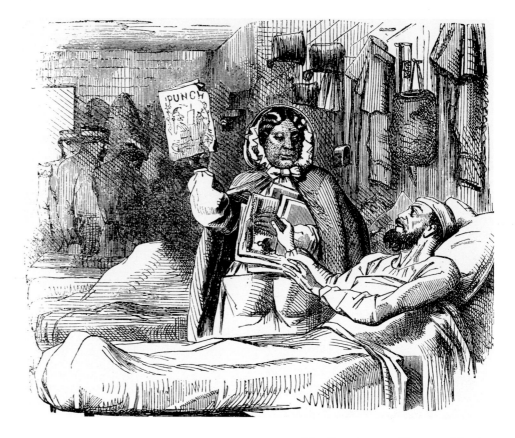

Mrs Seacole was well respected by the many soldiers she cared for in the Crimea. In this picture, she shows a copy of the magazine *Punch* to a wounded soldier.

She travelled everywhere, with her medicines on one mule and ham and wine on another, caring for the battle victims. She even went to the front, sometimes refusing to wait until a battle had ended before going among the dead and dying men, whether enemy or **ally**, giving them aid and comfort.

Her fame spread and when, at the end of the war, she returned to Britain almost penniless, a national fund was set up by well-wishers to help her out of her difficulties. A Grand Military Festival was organized for her benefit.

16

The Times of 28 July 1857 described the event:

'...Few names were more familiar to the public during the late war than that of Mrs Seacole... At the end of both the first and second parts the name of Mrs Seacole was shouted by a thousand voices... Never did woman seem happier, and never was hearty and kindly greeting bestowed upon a worthier object.'

The story she wrote of her life, *Wonderful Adventures of Mrs Seacole in Many Lands*, became a bestseller.

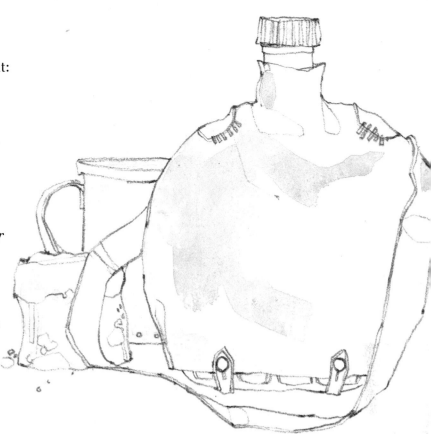

This is the front cover of Mrs Seacole's bestselling book about her life.

OTHER WOMEN DOCTORS AND NURSES

Florence Nightingale
– a nurse.
Elizabeth Garrett Anderson
– a physician and feminist.
Elizabeth Blackwell
– the first woman doctor.

Isambard Kingdom Brunel

1806 - 1859

'*We went down the shaft on the south bank, and got into a punt, which he was to steer into the tunnel... Brunel, swinging carelessly from right to left, fell overboard, and out went the candles with which he was lighting up the place... by the glimmering light from the entrance, we found young Brunel, who swam like a fish, coming up... and soon got him on board.*'

This describes Isambard Kingdom Brunel at the age of twenty taking a party of sightseers down into a tunnel flooded by river water. It clearly shows his fearless character. Brunel was

The Thames tunnel, built by Isambard Brunel and his father, Marc, was at first open to people on foot only. Later it was adapted for trains and is still in use today.

18

managing the construction of his father's tunnel under the Thames. This tunnel, nicknamed 'The Great Bore', took eighteen years to complete, mainly because the walls kept collapsing, letting in the river water.

After work on the tunnel had stopped, Brunel entered a competition to design a bridge across the River Avon at Bristol. His winning entry was eventually to become the great Clifton Suspension Bridge.

Compare this picture of Brunel's Clifton Suspension Bridge as it is today with the original design for it, below.

In the original design for the Clifton bridge the supporting towers were in the style of Egyptian temples, with sphinxes on top.

DATE CHART

1806
Isambard Kingdom Brunel is born.

1814
George Stephenson builds the first efficient steam locomotive.

1825
Work begins on the Thames tunnel.
George Stephenson builds *The Rocket*, a famous locomotive.

1826
Brunel becomes an engineer in charge of the tunnel works.

1830
Brunel's design is chosen for the Clifton Bridge.

1831
Construction of the Clifton Bridge begins.

Brunel then turned his mind to railways and won the job of **surveying** the land for the new railway to run between London and Bristol. The work had to be done on horseback and he was often riding for twenty hours a day. He was quite short but his personality and huge energy earned him the nickname of 'Little Giant'. There was a lot of opposition to the railway. The Duke of Wellington voiced the fears of many rich people when he expressed his worries that the railway 'would encourage the lower classes to move about.'

The 'Little Giant', standing in front of the huge chains used to control the launching of his unlucky steamship, the *Great Eastern*.

1833
Starts a survey for the Great Western Railway.

1836
Marriage to Mary Horsley.

1837
***Great Western* steamship is launched and crosses the Atlantic in fourteen and a half days.**

1841
Great Western Railway opens.

1843
Thames Tunnel opens. *Great Britain* steamship is launched.

1844
Bristol and Exeter Railway opens.

1854
Work on the *Great Eastern* begins.

1855
Designs and oversees the construction of a ready-made hospital for use in the Crimea.

1859
Royal Albert Bridge at Saltash is completed. *Great Eastern* explodes on its first voyage. Brunel dies.

Within a few years Brunel had built the biggest ship in the world, the *Great Western*, designed to cross the Atlantic Ocean. On its first voyage it caught fire, however, and Brunel fell down a deep hatch as he rushed to put out the blaze. He recovered and went on to build the first steamboat to be made of iron instead of wood. But it was his attempt to build a ship big enough to carry its own coal between Britain and Australia that was his downfall.

The *Great Eastern*, as it was called, had many problems and Brunel worried so much about it that he became ill. He was lying in bed, gravely ill, when the *Great Eastern* finally set off on its first voyage. But it exploded before it reached the open sea. Shortly after hearing this sad news, Brunel died.

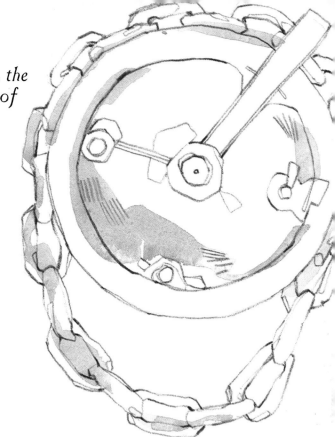

'By his death the greatest of England's engineers was lost, the man with the greatest originality of thought and power of execution, bold in his plans but right.'

So said his friend, the engineer Daniel Gooch. Yet this was not everyone's opinion at that time. An article written for *The Field* just months before, said:

'If great engineering consists in effecting huge monuments of folly (madness) at an enormous cost to shareholders, then is Mr Brunel surely the greatest of engineers ...'

Which view of the man do you think has more truth in it?

On the first voyage of the *Great Eastern*, an explosion wrecked much of the ship. It was repaired, however, and was used for laying cables across the Atlantic Ocean.

OTHER ENGINEERS

Joseph Locke
George Stephenson
Daniel Gooch
Robert Stephenson
– all railway engineers.

21

Charles Darwin

1809–1882

'There are many to whom Mr Darwin's death is a wholly irreparable loss. And this is not merely because of his wonderfully genial, simple, and generous nature; his cheerful and animated conversation, and the infinite variety and accuracy of his information; but because the more one knew of him, the more he seemed the incorporated ideal of a man of science.'

Darwin's friend and fellow 'man of science', Thomas Huxley, wrote this after Darwin's death in 1882.

Charles Darwin spent his life searching for the truth about the world through careful observation of nature. At the age of twenty-one

This portrait, by Julia Margaret Cameron (see pages 32-5), was taken when Darwin was fifty-eight years old.

22

he set off round the world as the official **naturalist** on a ship called the *Beagle*. He was fascinated by the extraordinary animals he saw and made a great collection of specimens to take home, including the **fossilized** bones of enormous animals that had died out long ago. The great variety of creatures he observed gave Darwin a new idea. He wrote in his journal:

'Both in space and time, we seem to be brought somewhat nearer to that great fact – that mystery of mysteries – the first appearance of new beings on this earth.'

Darwin went on a five-year voyage around the world aboard this ship, H.M.S. *Beagle*, collecting and observing plants and animals.

Darwin developed his idea into a theory over the next twenty years. He published it in a book called *The Origin of Species*. It was this theory – of **evolution** through **natural selection** – that caused an uproar at the time and has completely changed our way of looking at the world.

This vampire bat was one of the many strange animals that Darwin found on his travels.

The idea of evolution was not new. People realized that animals and plants had changed over thousands of years. But Darwin's theory gave a reason for the changes. He believed that animals and plants which were suited to their environment survived and bred while the rest died out. The offspring kept their parents' useful features and developed them, and the species gradually evolved.

In this page from his journal of the *Beagle* voyage, Darwin writes of the terrible storms that hit the ship off the southern tip of South America.

OTHER NATURALISTS

Thomas Huxley
– a biologist.
Henry Bates
– a zoologist.
Charles Lyell
– a geologist.
Alfred Wallace
– a biologist.
Joseph Hooker
– a botanist.

This theory was unpopular among people who believed, as it says in the *Bible*, that God created the world in six days. But what upset people most was the idea that humans had evolved as well, especially when Darwin suggested that their ancestors were apes.

Darwin did not mean to cause such a furious argument. He wrote:

'But we are not concerned with hopes and fears, only with the truth as far as our reason permits us to discover it.'

Darwin spent much of his life observing and recording as many different species of plant as he could find.

Soon after he came back from his voyage on the *Beagle*, he married his cousin, Emma. Darwin proved a very kind father to their ten children. His daughter, Henrietta, described him as

'... the most delightful play-fellow, and the most perfect sympathizer. Indeed it is impossible adequately to describe how delightful a relation he was to his family, whether as children or in their later lives.'

DATE CHART

1809
Charles Darwin is born.

1831–36
Darwin's voyage on the *Beagle*.

1839
Journal of the Voyage of the Beagle is published.
Marries his cousin, Emma Wedgwood.

1848
Henry Bates sets out for a seven-year trip to the Amazon. He collects 14,000 species of insect.

1859
The Origin of Species is published.

1871
The Descent of Man is published.

1881
Natural History Museum, London, opens.

1882
Darwin dies.

William Gladstone

1809 - 1898

'The ground on which we stand is not British, nor European, but it is human.'

William Gladstone said this in 1896 when the **British Empire** was at its height. It was an unpopular view, but Gladstone was never afraid to stand up for what he believed. Known as the 'Grand Old Man' of British politics, he was a member of the **House of Commons** for sixty years and Prime Minister four times.

One of Gladstone's greatest achievements was the Irish Land Act of 1881. This act protected Irish tenants from the exploitation by their landlords (many of whom were English) which they had suffered for centuries. This cartoon shows Gladstone as a knight in shining armour.

OTHER POLITICIANS

Robert Peel
Benjamin Disraeli
– Tory Prime Ministers.
James Keir Hardie
– the first leader of the Labour Party.
Joseph Chamberlain
– a Liberal politician.

26

Gladstone believed that Ireland should govern itself, not be ruled by England. It was an unpopular view and this cartoon shows him (with his Irish Home Rule Bill in his hat) being kicked out of Parliament by other Members of Parliament.

In the nineteenth century there were two main political parties, the Tories (an early version of the present-day Conservatives) and the Liberals, or Whigs, as they were called. When Gladstone first became a Member of Parliament he was considered 'the rising hope of the stern unbending Tories'. But in the course of his career he found himself sympathizing more and more with the views of the Liberals. He ended up as leader of the Liberal party, 'the peoples' William', dreaded by the Queen and the upper classes for his **radicalism**. He supported the Reform Bills which gave the right to vote to almost all men instead of just a privileged few. Queen Victoria wrote:

'Lord Palmerston was quite right when he said to me "Mr Gladstone is a very dangerous man". And so arrogant, tyrannical and obstinate with no knowledge of the world or human nature.'

Gladstone was a very religious man. He kept records and journals of everything he did, which filled seventy-five volumes. He chewed each mouthful of food thirty-two times and he was so long-winded that he could speak for several hours without stopping. He was a great **orator**, able to inspire his audiences and stir up popular feeling. Above all, he stood out from other politicians because of his determination to do what he felt was morally right.

DATE CHART

1809
William Ewart Gladstone is born.

1832
Elected a Tory MP.
First Reform Bill gives the vote to middle-class men.

1859
Becomes Chancellor of the Exchequer in Palmerston's Liberal government.

1865
Becomes Prime Minister (Liberal).

1867
Second Reform Bill gives the vote to working-class men in towns.

1874
Defeated in the general election.

1880
Becomes Prime Minister again.

1884
Third Reform Bill gives the vote to men in the country.

1885
Re-elected as Prime Minister.

1886
First Irish Home Rule Bill. The Bill is lost and Gladstone resigns.

1892
Becomes Prime Minister again.

1893
Second Home Rule Bill is passed by the House of Commons but is rejected by the House of Lords.

1898
William Gladstone dies.

27

Charles Dickens

1812–1870

'No words can express the secret agony of my soul ... I mixed my tears with the water in which I was washing the bottles.'

This twelve-year-old boy was working in a filthy, rat-infested **blacking** warehouse. He had no hopes of education or a bright future. He was living in bleak, depressing lodgings, seeing his family only on Sundays. His father had been imprisoned for debt and his mother and younger brothers and sisters were in jail with him. The boy's name was Charles Dickens.

Dickens posting his first manuscript.

For the rest of his life Dickens kept secret the horrors of his childhood. But it was from his memories that Dickens created many of the characters and stories of his sixteen novels. At first, his stories were **serialized** in magazines and soon they became very popular. Everyone waited anxiously for the next issue to find out what happened next.

Dickens showed his concern for other people by helping the wounded in the Staplehurst rail crash in 1865.

DATE CHART

1812
Charles Dickens is born in Portsea.

1824
His father is imprisoned for debt; Charles goes to work in a blacking warehouse.

1827
Becomes a solicitor's clerk.

1829–33
Works as a law court/parliamentary reporter.

1833–5
Writes sketches using the name Boz.

1836–70
Writes his sixteen novels.

1837
The first of his ten children is born.

1842
Visits the USA and publishes *American Notes.*

The stories were often very sad, describing the tragic lives of children growing up in the terrible conditions which were common at that time. Readers felt sorry for the characters as if they were real. In Dickens' novel *The Old Curiosity Shop*, the heroine, Nell, dies at the end. The actor William Macready wrote in his diary that he:

'Called on Dickens . . . Asked Dickens to spare the life of Nell in his story, and observed that he was cruel. He blushed.'

This picture shows Dickens in his study, dreaming up the characters and stories of his books.

Everyone felt sorry for the characters Oliver Twist, Little Nell and Paul Dombey. This made them want to do something about all the real children who led such unhappy lives. Because the novels became so popular, everyone learnt about the cruelty and injustice of Victorian society. Gradually laws were passed that helped to improve people's lives and protect children.

Queen Victoria wrote in her diary two days after Dickens' death:

'He had a large loving mind and the strongest sympathy with the poorer classes. He felt sure a better feeling, and much greater union of classes would take place in time. And I pray earnestly it may.'

Dickens' stories are still popular today. Here is a still from a recent film of *Little Dorrit* (below). It shows the same scene as this original nineteenth-century title page (left).

OTHER MALE AUTHORS

William Thackeray
Anthony Trollope
Charles Kingsley
Wilkie Collins
Thomas Hardy
– all novelists.

Julia Margaret Cameron

1815 – 1879

'I longed to arrest all beauty that came before me.'

When she was given her first camera at the age of forty-eight, Julia Margaret Cameron was finally able to capture this beauty. From that moment on there was no stopping her. Friends, passing children, servants, people in the street – if she thought them beautiful she would insist that they come to her studio and pose for her camera.

Julia Cameron lived on the Isle of Wight to be near her great friends, the poet Alfred, Lord Tennyson and his wife. She was very generous, always giving presents to her friends. The poet Henry Taylor said that she was:

'... one of the most benevolent of human beings, always thinking of something for the good and pleasure of others.'

A magnesium torch like this was used by early photographers to create enough light to get a good picture.

A portrait of Julia Margaret Cameron.

Julia Cameron's behaviour and clothes were unusual. She dressed in loose, flowing robes and Indian shawls, with her hands, and sometimes clothes, blackened by photographic chemicals. Garibaldi, the great Italian hero, 'thought she was a beggar when she kneeled before him, begging to take his picture', and waved her away.

In the nineteeth century, most photographic studios took very formal, boring portraits of people.

33

Her portraits show her 'longing' to record 'the greatness of the inner as well as the outer man'. This is one of the reasons why her pictures are so different from most of the photographs of the time. Portraits were generally dull and did not show the personality of the sitter. One critic wrote of her photographs:

'The portraits are about half the size of life, and are remarkable for force and tenderness of expression and a classical effectiveness never attained in photographs before.'

Ellen Terry, the famous Victorian actress, photographed by Julia Margaret Cameron as a young woman.

The French author Victor Hugo, writing to thank her for some photographs, was very enthusiastic:

'All of them are beautiful, not one of the photographs but is in itself a masterpiece. No one has ever captured the rays of the Sun and used them as you have. I throw myself at your feet.'

34

Julia Margaret Cameron was one of the first Victorians to use the camera imaginatively. She is now regarded not only as a pioneer photographer but also as one of the best British artists of the nineteenth century. She died in Ceylon (now Sri Lanka) in 1879, looking through the open window at a clear night sky. Her last word was 'beautiful'.

Mrs Cameron took a series of these pictures to illustrate Tennyson's poem about King Arthur, *The Passing of Arthur*.

35

OTHER PHOTOGRAPHERS

Lewis Carroll
– a writer.
Frank Meadows Sutcliffe
Edweard Muybridge
– pioneer photographers.

Charlotte Brontë

1816 – 1855

'Finished Jane Eyre which is really a wonderful book, very peculiar in parts, but so powerfully and admirably written, such a fine tone it is, such fine religious feeling, and such beautiful writings...'

Queen Victoria wrote this in her journal. Yet many people considered the book to be wicked and were shocked by the story. It is about a young **governess**, Jane Eyre, who falls in love with her employer, Mr Rochester. He has a dark secret which is revealed towards the end of the book.

As children, the Brontës had an imaginary world called 'Glass Town' which was full of interesting characters having exciting adventures. They wrote tiny books about it in minute writing.

Charlotte Brontë used her own experiences when she wrote *Jane Eyre*. But her novel has a happier ending than her own life story. She lived in a remote **parsonage** on a windswept Yorkshire moor with her father, brother and sisters. All the children were infected with **tuberculosis** and all died young. Their short lives were dull, cheered up only by books and their own imaginations.

Charlotte and her two sisters, Emily and Anne, wrote many novels under the **pseudonyms** Currer, Ellis and Acton Bell. They knew their work would be judged more fairly by Victorian society if they pretended to be men. Their books, especially Charlotte's *Jane Eyre*, and *Wuthering Heights* by Emily Brontë, are still popular today. Charlotte wrote three novels – *Jane Eyre*, *Shirley* and *Villette*.

Everyone was surprised to find that the real Currer Bell was a very small, shy Yorkshire woman.

Compare the portrait of Charlotte, drawn in 1850, with this description by her friend, the novelist Elizabeth Gaskell:

'She is (as she calls herself) underdeveloped; thin and more than half a head shorter than I, soft brown hair . . . ; eyes (very good and expressive looking straight and open at you) of the same colour, a reddish face; large mouth, and many teeth gone; altogether plain; the forehead square, broad, and rather overhanging. She has a very sweet voice . . .'

The artist Richmond sketched flattering pictures of many famous Victorians. Do you think his portrait (above) is honest?

OTHER WOMEN AUTHORS

Elizabeth Gaskell
Jane Austen
George Eliot
– all novelists.

Emily Davies
1830 - 1921

'Her dainty little figure and smiling face were most misleading: they concealed untiring energy, a will of iron and a very clear and definite set of opinions.'

Emily Davies was a young Victorian woman in a very common situation. With neither the beauty nor money to assure her of marriage, she was destined to stay at home and serve her family. However, this frustrated her and she decided to do something for all women.

Emily's only education was very basic lessons from her mother. But she did not want to stay at home doing needlework and making polite conversation as other young women were made to do. She used to wander

It is thanks to Emily Davies and her dream of a college for women that women now have the opportunity to go to university.

38

secretly through the streets of Gateshead. She was not afraid of walking in the backstreets and soon got to know the slums and the very poor people who lived there. She was shocked by their terrible living conditions and especially worried about the women she met.

Later on she was to write:

'Working-class women are undernourished, constantly sick, old before their time, worn out by child-bearing, ill-treatment and work that is far too heavy.'

She said that these women should be taught a skill so that they could have paid work. She believed strongly that 'self-help not charity is what is needed'. She felt that all women should be educated, so they could have jobs and independence.

Many people thought that women should not go to university. This is a demonstration in Cambridge against women receiving degrees, nearly thirty years after Girton was founded.

DATE CHART

1830
Emily Davies is born in Southampton.

1860
Moves to London with her mother.

1863
Girls sit the Local examinations for the first time.

1868
Gives evidence for the Royal Commission on Girls' Schools.

1869
Hitchin College is founded. *Higher Education for Women* is published.

When her father died, when she was thirty, Emily was able to begin the work that became her lifelong obsession. With her friends Elizabeth Garrett (who was to become the first British woman doctor) and Barbara Bodichon, a leading **feminist**, she worked on the *English Woman's Journal*. This journal encouraged the open discussion of women's rights.

Emily believed passionately in the need and right for women to be educated. Above all, she had a dream of a university college for women. But she had to overcome the doubts of many women as well as men. One worried mother explained her fear:

'What should I do if my daughter should return from college and address me in Latin or Greek?'

Some people suggested that women were not strong enough to cope with the mental strain of studying and exams. Emily replied angrily in a letter to *The Times*:

'... is it because of a poor woman's lack of strength that they are employed as beasts of burden in mines and factories and are condemned to sweated labour from the age of six...?'

To begin with, Emily organized the first girls to sit the Local examinations. Until then, these had been open only to boys. The success of the girls quietened Emily's opponents who had said that girls were not as clever as boys and not worth educating. It also helped her to raise the support and money needed to found a university college for women.

Emily Davies's dream came true in 1873, when Girton College, Cambridge, was founded.

Miss Johnson, who had beaten all the male Cambridge students in the final maths exams, is 'chaired' by fellow students.

The five original students at her college did so well that by 1873 Emily was able to build Girton College at Cambridge.

Emily insisted that her students be treated just the same as the men, that they follow the same courses of study and take the same exams. And she was proved right, because the success of those female students helped to prove that women were just as clever as men. This eventually led to the opening up of all universities to women.

Since Girton was founded, more and more women are going to university. In 1992, 47 per cent (just under half) of the students starting university were women.

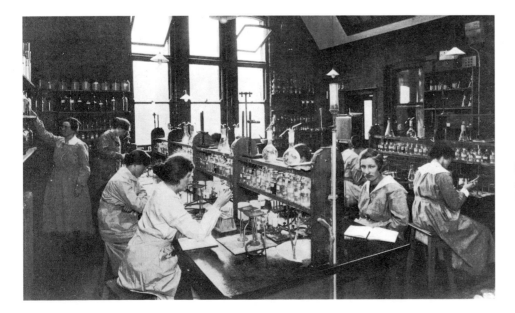

Women at work in the laboratory of natural sciences at Girton in 1931.

OTHER EDUCATION REFORMERS

Robert Owen
– an industrialist.
William Forster
– a founder of primary schools.
Frances Mary Buss
Dorothea Beale
– pioneers of women's education.

Mary Kingsley

1862-1900

'And very glad I shall be to hear my own drum name again when slipping in a canoe past a village which may never have seen my face. Very sincerely shall I thump back my answering – "friends may you live for ever ..."'

Mary Kingsley, unlike most other travellers in Africa in the nineteenth century, not only loved the country but also valued the people highly. She strongly criticized the Christian **missionaries** from Britain who forced their own culture and religion upon the African people. She believed that

Cartoons of Mary Kingsley drawn by students in one of her lectures. On the left is how they expected her to be, on the right, something closer to the truth.

42

Mary Kingsley, seated in the middle, in Nigeria. She did not like Europeans who wanted to impose their own way of life on to African people.

the Africans' own religion and way of life should be respected, and when newspapers portrayed Africans as savage and violent, she replied:

'... you will not see in a whole year on the Coast (of Africa) one seventieth part of the evil, degradation, and premature decay you can see any afternoon you like to take a walk in the densely populated parts of any of our towns.'

Most of Mary Kingsley's life was spent as a loyal daughter serving her family. Soon after her parents died, however, Mary left for Africa. Her travels took her to the heart of the continent. She climbed to the peak of Mount Cameroon and travelled up the Congo River. She sailed through the whirlpools of Hell's Cauldron, which spun the ship round like a canoe. She collected specimens and often had to hit over-friendly crocodiles on the nose with her parasol. She wrote:

'I asked one of my Adjuma crew if there were many gorillas, elephants, leopards, and bush-cow round here? "Plenty too much," said he, and I wished myself in England, at the same time regretfully remembering that the last word a scientific friend had said to me before I left home was, "Always take measurements, Miss Kingsley, and always from the adult male".'

DATE CHART

1862
Mary Henrietta Kingsley is born.

1892
Mary's father and mother die.
August: Visits the Canary Islands.

1893
Visits Africa.

1894
Visits Africa again.
May: Sails up the Ogooue River and leads her first expedition.
August: Visits Corisco Island.
September: Begins climbing Mount Cameroon.
November: Returns to Britain.

1897
Travels in West Africa is published.

1899
West African Studies is published.

1900
The Story of West Africa is published.
Goes to the Boer War as a nurse.
June: Dies of typhoid.

OTHER EXPLORERS

Dr Livingstone
John Speke
Richard Burton
Henry Stanley

43

Glossary

Ally A friend in wartime.

Apprentice Someone who learns a trade.

Blacking A substance used to blacken shoes, metal, etc.

British Empire The overseas territories which were controlled by Britain.

Cholera A dangerous disease carried in water polluted by sewage.

Crimean War A war between Russia and the combined powers of Turkey, Britain and France (1853-56).

Dynamo A machine that generates electricity by rotating coils of copper wire in a magnetic field.

Electromagnet A magnet made using electricity.

Evolution In biology, the process by which life has developed on the earth.

Expatiate To speak or write at great length about something.

Feminist Someone who believes that women should have equal rights to men.

Fossilized Turned into fossils.

Fossils The remains (often bones, teeth, shells) of once-living things which have been preserved in rock since prehistoric times.

Governess A woman who teaches children in their own home.

House of Commons A group of Members of Parliament in the British Parliament.

Malaria A disease, common in many parts of the world, spread by a type of mosquito.

Member of Parliament Someone who is elected to represent people in Parliament.

Missionaries People who were sent to other countries by the Christian Church. They wanted to spread their religious beliefs all around the world.

Naturalist A person who studies animals, plants and other aspects of nature.

Natural selection The way in which certain types of plant or animal survive while others die out.

Orator A good public speaker.

Parsonage The house where a parson or vicar lives.

Pseudonym A false name used by an author.

Quaker A member of the Society of Friends, a religious group.

Radicalism A political movement which hopes to change society greatly.

School Boards Groups of people who made sure there were schools for all the children in their area.

Serialized Told in parts, like a television soap opera.

Smallpox A dangerous disease which, due to vaccination, has now died out.

Surveying Carefully measuring and recording the features of the land.

Sutler Someone who sells food and other provisions to armies.

Tuberculosis A disease which killed many people in the nineteenth century.

Vaccinate To give someone a mild form of virus for protection against a disease.

Books to read

M. Brophy, *Michael Faraday* (Wayland, 1990)
A. Evans, *Victorian Law and Order* (Batsford, 1988)
N. Hunter, *Charles Dickens* (Wayland, 1988)
K. Hyndley, *The Voyage of the Beagle* (Wayland, 1989)
M. Jones, *The Poor in Nineteenth Century Britain* (Batsford, 1986)
M. Moss, *The Victorians* (Wayland, 1986)
S. Parker, *Charles Darwin and Evolution* (Belitha Press, 1992)

M. Rawcliffe, *Victorian Public Health and Housing* (Batsford, 1987)
M. Rawcliffe, *Victorian Social Reformers* (Batsford, 1987)
P. Speed, *Learning and Teaching in Victorian Times* (Longman, 1988)
A. Steel, *Victorian Children* (Wayland, 1989)
T. Triggs, *Victorian Britain* (Wayland, 1990)

Places to visit

Elizabeth Fry
Beaumaris Gaol, Beaumaris, Gwynedd. Tel: (0535) 642323
Royal London Hospital Museum, Newark Street, London. Tel: (071) 377 7000

Michael Faraday
Science Museum, South Kensington, London. Tel: (071) 938 8000

Mary Seacole
Royal London Hospital Museum (see above)

Isambard Kingdom Brunel
British Engineerium, Hove, East Sussex. Tel: (0273) 559583
Great Western Railway Museum, Swindon, Wiltshire. Tel: (0793) 526161 extension 4552
Ironbridge Gorge Museum, Ironbridge, Telford. Tel: (0952) 433522
National Railway Museum, York. Tel: (0904) 621261
SS. *Great Britain*, Great Western Dock, Bristol. Tel: (0272) 260680

Charles Darwin
Darwin Museum, Downe House, Downe, Orpington, Kent. Tel: (0689) 859119
Natural History Museum, South Kensington, London. Tel: (071) 938 9123

William Gladstone
Down Museum, Downpatrick, Co. Down. Tel: (0396) 5218
Museum of London, London Wall. Tel: (071) 600 3699

Charles Dickens
Dickens House, Doughty Street, London. Tel: (071) 405 2127
Dickens House Museum, Broadstairs, Kent. Tel: (0843) 62853

Julia Margaret Cameron
National Museum of Film, Photography and TV, Bradford, Yorkshire. Tel: (0274) 727488

Charlotte Brontë
Brontë Parsonage Museum, Haworth, West Yorkshire. Tel: (0535) 642323

Emily Davies
Plunket Museum of Irish Education, Dublin. Tel: (01) 970033
Ragged School Museum, Copperfield Road, London. Tel: (081) 980 6405
Scotland Street School, Museum of Education, Glasgow. Tel: (041) 429 1202

Mary Kingsley
National Maritime Museum, Greenwich, London. Tel: (081) 858 4422
Natural History Museum (see above)

Index